Bamburgh Castle is built on a north-easterly outcrop of The Great Whin Sill, an intrusion of volcanic rock covering almost 4,000 square kilometres of the north of England. Standing on its rocky plateau 45m above sea level, it dominates the present-day village and has uninterrupted views out to sea of Holy Island and the Farnes. With such clear defensive potential, it would be strange if it had not been a place of fortification from the earliest times.

The first visitors of whom there is evidence were not, however, primarily interested in such matters...

Mesolithic Period:
10,000 – 4,000 BC

Archaeologists have found a number of arrowheads and small flint tools called microliths in the Bamburgh area. The people who made them were nomadic hunter-gatherers, following the herds of wild animals, which roamed the area. They probably also came down to the sea to fish and to collect shellfish from the shore. The earliest permanent settlement would have occurred in…

The Neolithic ('New Stone Age')

This period has been described as the greatest social revolution in human history, marked by the beginning of farming and of the domestication of animals. In Britain it occurred relatively late, from about 3,500 to 2,500 BC. With farming, the land was divided up for the first time between families and tribes. In Bamburgh, the evidence of a settlement has yet to be discovered, but in 1897 a stone axe head was found in a field near the village. This suggests that there was occupation which continued into…

The Bronze Age:
2,400 – 700BC

Excavations during the 19th century in a large mound just south of the castle uncovered the stone-lined grave of a man, 1.7m (5'6") tall and a pottery vessel, apparently from different Bronze Age burials.

The Iron Age:
700BC – AD43

During the 1960's and 70's, some excavation by Dr Brian Hope-Taylor in the West Ward of the present castle yielded pottery sherds, the earliest of which were dated to the Iron Age.

The Roman Occupation:
AD43 – AD410

It is unknown what impact the coming of the Romans probably had on Bamburgh, but for the first time we begin to find written evidence pertaining to the inhabitants of Britain. It is often forgotten that the Romans several times advanced into Scotland beyond the River Forth before eventually drawing back to Hadrian's Wall which is, of course, south of Bamburgh. Thus the lands of the local tribe, the Votadini, were alternately occupied and abandoned by the Romans: ultimately it would appear that they became a client-kingdom of the Romans, left very much to their own devices. A chronicler in the 8th century tells us that the British name of Bamburgh was Dynguoaroy, which suggests that by this time it was a fortress of some importance.

Early Medieval: AD411–AD1066
The Coming of the Anglo-Saxons

In AD 540, the British monk Gildas wrote an impassioned account of the arrival, a century before, of settlers from Denmark, Frisia and Germany which was called De Excidio Britanniae or 'The Ruin of Britain'. In it he accuses the rulers of Britain of inviting in

'the fierce and impious Saxons, a race hateful to both God and men'

to fight against the northern tribes. They expanded north and west through Britain, establishing new kingdoms. The Anglian king, Ida, arrived in Bamburgh and took over the Celtic Kingdom of Bryneich: The Venerable Bede, writing around AD 730, tells us that

'in the year 547, Ida began to reign'

Further information is provided by The Anglo-Saxon Chronicles which tell us that

'He reigned for twelve years, and built Bamburgh, which was at first enclosed by a stockade, then a wall.'

This drawing of an Anglo-Saxon man was based on a facial reconstruction of one of the skeletons discovered by the Bamburgh Research Project. The King's Hall (below), in Anglo-Saxon times. Both drawn for BBC's Meet the Ancestors programme by Jane Brayne, archaeological illustrator.

The citadel would have been quite unlike that of the later stone castle that we see today, its timber defences and single storey buildings lending it a very different appearance. These defences were, according to Bede, later attacked by King Penda of Mercia who attempted to burn them down in AD 651. However, the story goes, Bishop Aidan saw the flames from his monastery on Lindisfarne. He prayed for Penda's defeat, upon which the wind changed direction and blew the smoke and flames back towards the invaders.

There would have been a large timber hall surrounded by a number of smaller timber buildings. Such a hall, the Hall of Heorot, is described in the Anglo-Saxon epic poem Beowulf which some scholars believe to have been composed by a Northumbrian court poet in the 7th or 8th century, maybe at Bamburgh itself?

Northumbria's Saint-Kings

The heir to the neighbouring kingdom of Deira, Edwin, was only an infant when his father died in AD589 and his uncle, Ethelric, took the throne. In AD604, King Ethelric died and his son, Ethelfrith, who was king of Bernicia succeeded him, thus uniting the two kingdoms into the kingdom of Northumbria. It is he, supposedly, who changed the name Dynguoaroy to Bebbanburgh in honour of his wife, Bebba. In time, this became Bamburgh. The dispossessed Edwin eventually raised sufficient support to confront and kill Ethelfrith at the Battle of the River Idle in AD616. Edwin's second marriage in AD625 was to Ethelburga, sister of the Christian king of Kent, upon which he agreed to embrace her religion, thus becoming the first Christian king of Northumbria. He brought Paulinus, a companion of Augustine - who was the missionary sent to Britain by Pope Gregory - to Northumbria to convert his people. Although based in York, Bamburgh remained an important stronghold for him. We know that he entertained Paulinus at the royal palace of Yeavering which is about 20 miles from Bamburgh. He was killed in battle in AD633 by King Penda of Mercia: as Penda was not a Christian, Edwin was regarded as a martyr and was eventually canonised, becoming St Edwin. On the death of their father, King Ethelfrith's children fled into exile for safety. The second eldest of these, Oswald, together with his brother Oswiu, were sent

to be educated by the Irish monks of Iona where they were baptised. Oswald returned to Northumbria and was proclaimed king. In AD634 he defeated and killed Cadwallon, King of Gwynnedd, at the Battle of Heavenfield, just north of Hexham. In AD638 he may have extended the kingdom northwards by capturing Dyn Eidin, now Edinburgh. By the end of his reign, Bede claims that he had established himself as overlord of almost the whole of Britain, ruling from Bamburgh.

At this time there were two distinct interpretations of Christianity in Britain. The one which Paulinus had brought to the north under King Edwin was that of Rome but Oswald had been introduced to the faith through the Celtic tradition as practised at Iona. Perhaps discomfited by what he could well have seen as heresy in his new kingdom, he asked the abbot of Iona to send him a missionary: the person he got was Aidan. Aidan, it is said, spoke only Gaelic and King Oswald often acted as his interpreter. In AD635, he gave to Aidan land on Lindisfarne in sight of the royal citadel, on which to found the monastery which was to become one of the foremost seats of learning in Europe. Oswald became noted for his piety and charity. The legend is that on being informed of a number of beggars at the gate, he lifted the silver dish heaped with meat and gave it to them. Aidan, who was present, prayed that the arm which did this should never decay. When, in AD642, Oswald was defeated in battle against the old enemy of Northumbria, Penda, his corpse was dismembered. His men were able to rescue his head and his arms and bring them home to Bamburgh: his head was interred at Lindisfarne but Bede tells us that his arms were placed in a silver shrine in the Church of St Peter

'in the royal city which has taken its name from Bebba, one of its former queens'.

Thus Oswald became a saint and Aidan, who died at Bamburgh in AD651, was in due course also canonised.

The kingdom of Northumbria by now extended from Edinburgh to Leeds, and continued for a further 225 years after the death of Oswald with the focus of power shifting periodically between Bamburgh and York.

The Archaeological Evidence

A fragment of worked stone, broken in two, was discovered in the grounds of the castle in the 19th century. The carvings on it clearly dated it to the Anglo-Saxon period and it was thought to be part of a stone cross until it was re-appraised in the latter part of the 20th century by Professor Rosemary Cramp of Durham University. She identified it as the arm of a stone chair similar to those thought to serve as bishops' thrones at the monasteries of Hexham and Beverley. However, being in a secular but royal setting, it is thought that this may be have been part of the throne of the Northumbrian kings.

During Dr Brian Hope-Taylor's excavations of the West Ward in the 1960's and 70's he discovered, among other things, Anglian coins, a sword and, potentially evidence of metalworking. This is not surprising in the context of a royal citadel; besides the obvious need for weaponry and domestic items the custom of giving jewellery, and particularly rings, was an important aspect of Anglo-Saxon society. The king would present the gifts publicly from his throne; to accept them was a binding token of fealty. Perhaps Hope-Taylor's single most evocative discovery was the gold plaque, which is affectionately known as 'The Bamburgh Beast'.

In 1816/7, a great storm blew away part of the sand dunes to the east of the castle, revealing a number of cists. These are stone-lined graves, sometimes covered with a stone slab. Right up to the 1930's, archaeologists carried out examination of the site, but no records of these excavations survive and in time even the exact location of the cemetery was forgotten. In 1998 the site, which has come to be known as The Bowl Hole Cemetery, was re-discovered by the Bamburgh Research Project. From the excavations to date it is clear that the burials date from the 7th and 8th centuries, the time of Oswald and his successors. Scientific analysis of differing trace elements within the teeth of the skeletons can tell us where a person grew up. Of the skeletons tested so far, half grew up in the Bamburgh area. Of the rest, most had grown up in northern England or southern Scotland – within the kingdom of Northumbria. Two however came from further afield. One man seems to have lived his early life in northern Ireland or the Hebrides, the places where Oswald had spent his years in exile. Another woman had been brought up in central Norway, around the Trondheim area.

Signs on the bones show that all of the people had been tall, strong and well fed during their lives, all of which suggests that the Bowl Hole was a high-status burial site of the Northumbrian aristocracy.

More recent work by the Bamburgh Research Project has established the existence of an earlier building beneath the present 12th century chapel, possibly part of a range of buildings of the early fortress.

The Coming of the Norsemen

The entry for the year AD793 in the Anglo-Saxon Chronicles tells of 'fierce, foreboding omens' seen over Northumbria.

'There were excessive whirlwinds, lightning storms, and fiery dragons were seen flying in the sky.'

After great famine,

'the ravaging of heathen men destroyed God's church at Lindisfarne'.

This was the first major Viking attack on England; the first of many. We can only marvel at the temerity of the raiders who destroyed the monastery under the very noses of the Bamburgh garrison. Despite repeated attempts by the kings of Wessex and Mercia to buy off the invaders with what came to be known as 'danegeld', the raids became more frequent and more intense. A Viking army spent the winter of AD850 on English soil at the mouth of the River Thames; in

AD865 a 'Great Army' landed in East Anglia and swept through into Mercia; York fell in AD866 and AD867 saw the appointment of the first sub-king of Northumbria under Norse rule, Ecgberht I. This did not, however, spell the end for Bamburgh. Despite losing what was effectively the old kingdom of Deira, a family of High Reeves continued to rule from here an Anglo-Saxon Northumbria which extended from the River Forth to as far south as the River Tees. They remained in power until after the Norman Conquest. However, the monks of Lindisfarne had had enough. In AD875 they fled, taking with them their treasures which included the body of St Cuthbert and the head of St Oswald. It was to be many years before these were to find a permanent resting place in Durham Cathedral.

The Later Medieval: The Norman Conquest – 1066

After his success at the Battle of Hastings established him on the English throne, William soon recognised the importance of Northumbria as a buffer against the aggressive Scots. In an attempt to secure the allegiance of the Earl of Bamburgh, he confirmed his rights and privileges, thereby recognising the unique independence of Northumbria. It is significant that there are no entries for Northumberland or Durham in the Domesday Book.

Eventually, William determined to place one of his own men, Robert Comine, at Bamburgh but on his way there, Comine and his 700 strong army were massacred at Durham. William was so incensed that he led his army in a merciless attack on Northumbria. He then installed Waltheof, a member of the family of the Anglo-Saxon Bamburgh earls who had remained loyal, as Earl of Northumberland, marrying him to his niece Judith in order to further secure his loyalty. It proved to be a mistake. In 1075, Waltheof joined the Earls of Hereford and Norfolk in a rebellion which was quickly crushed. Waltheof threw himself on William's mercy. He was imprisoned for a year while William decided what to do with him before being executed on the orders of Bishop Odo of Bayeux during the king's absence. This presumably was to forestall any softening by the king towards his nephew-in-law. Further devastations of the north' followed, led by Bishop Odo, and for twenty years Northumbria was kept in uneasy subservience.

1464 spelt the end for castles: gunpowder and shot had proved stronger than stone and mortar.

In 1095, King William Rufus besieged Bamburgh Castle by building a siege castle known as a 'malvoisin' or 'evil neighbour'. It lay close enough to the castle for the defenders to shout abuse at the workers during its construction, but its location is not now known. The Earl of Northumbria, Robert de Mowbray, was forced to yield. The castle and the Earl's estates were forfeit to the Crown and Bamburgh passed into the ownership of the King. The threat from the Scots was still very real and Bamburgh's fortifications were modernised and strengthened in preparation for its new role as a garrison of the Borders. For the next 350 years it stood as one of the most northerly outposts of English rule, playing host to a succession of kings including John, Henry III, Edward I, Edward II and Edward III. Its most famous commander was Henry Percy, better known as Harry Hotspur. In it were imprisoned, at various times, Piers de Gaveston, Welsh princes captured during the conquest of Wales and David Bruce of Scotland.

The Wars of the Roses

These were a series of civil wars fought between the supporters of King Henry VI of the House of Lancaster and the later King Edward IV of the House of York between 1455 and 1487. Bamburgh Castle, together with nearby Dunstanburgh and Alnwick, was held for the king by the Lancastrians and it was from here that Henry attempted to continue to rule after his defeat at the Battle of Hexham in May, 1464. The following month, however, the Yorkist forces under the Earl of Warwick laid siege to Bamburgh, bringing with them heavy artillery, and Bamburgh acquired the dubious distinction of being the first castle in England to be destroyed by gunfire.

An interesting facet of the siege is that Warwick was accompanied by Sir Thomas Malory who was later to elaborate on the stories of King Arthur in his romance Le Morte d'Arthur. In this he says of Joyous Gard, the castle of Sir Launcelot, that 'some men say (it is) Alnwick and some men say Bamborow'; and so Bamburgh became part of the legend.

1464 spelt the end for castles: gunpowder and shot had proved stronger than stone and mortar. It was not considered worthwhile to re-fortify Bamburgh and, although retained by the king for its strategic potential, it was largely left quietly to decay for the next 230 years.

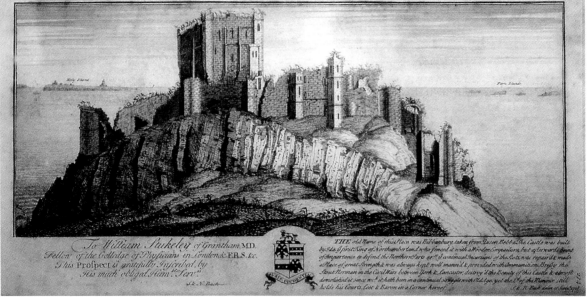

THE SOUTH-WEST VIEW OF BAMBURGH CASTLE IN NORTHUMBERLAND

AD1600 to the Present Day

The Forsters

Claudius Forster had been appointed Constable of Bamburgh towards the end of the reign of Elizabeth I and had served as Warden of the Marches. In recognition of his services, Bamburgh appears to have been given to him by James I who must have been delighted with the arrangement: a satisfied retainer for the cost of a semi-derelict castle which, now that Scotland and England were united, had no foreseeable defensive significance.

The Borders, however, remained lawless territory in which theft, arson and cattle-stealing were commonplace. The Forsters' principal talents appear to have been losing money and backing the wrong side. Before the end of the century, they were living at Bamburgh Manor, the castle being now uninhabitable. The direct line of the Bamburgh Forsters came to an end with Ferdinando, who died without issue during a duel in 1701. What little remained of the Bamburgh estates now fell to his sister and young nephew, Dorothy and Thomas, of the Adderstone branch of the family. Dorothy had made an advantageous marriage to Lord Nathaniel Crewe, Bishop of Durham. Lord Crewe was extremely wealthy and bought back the bankrupt Forster estates of Bamburgh and also Blanchland (which they had acquired by marriage in 1623).

At the age of 32, Tom joined the Jacobite uprising of 1715 but was captured and imprisoned in Newgate Gaol. The story of his rescue by his sister, also a Dorothy, was popularised by the 19th century novelist Walter Besant. The story goes that she rode pillion to London behind the Adderstone village blacksmith (whom she later married). There, after some business involving disguise and duplicate keys, she was successful in rescuing her brother and bringing him back to Bamburgh where she kept him hidden for two years until he was able to escape safely to France.

The Lord Crewe Trust

Lord Crewe died without heir in 1722. The terms of his will established a trust for the benefit of local charities which is still in existence today. One of the most energetic of the Trustees was Dr John Sharp, later Archdeacon of Northumberland, who is recorded as augmenting the Trust with large sums of his own money in the repair and upkeep of the Castle. Besides repairs to the Keep, he converted some parts of the buildings into granaries from which, when times were hard, corn could be sold to the poor at a fair price. The windmill built to grind the corn for the poor still stands in the west ward of the castle. After his death

in 1792 the work of the trustees continued and a visitor writing in 1835 tells us that 'A large room is fitted up for educating boys on the Madras system. A suite of rooms are also allotted to two mistresses and twenty poor girls, who from their ninth year are lodged, clothed and educated here till fit for service.' The writer goes on to enumerate the other charitable activities focused on the Castle, from lifeboat activities to an infirmary and dispensary which treated an average of 1,000 patients a year.

Lord Armstrong

William George Armstrong was born in 1810 in Newcastle. His father was a corn merchant and young William was destined for a career in law, but his first love was engineering and in 1847 he set up a works at Elswick . One of his most important inventions was the Armstrong breech-loading gun and he was appointed engineer to the War Department and given a knighthood. By 1882, his company had expanded into shipbuilding and was the biggest employer on Tyneside. The firm was eventually to become Vickers-Armstrong.

Lord Armstrong is perhaps best remembered for building Cragside near Rothbury, the first house in Britain to be lit by hydro-electricity. In the 1890's he purchased Bamburgh Castle and set about its extensive restoration which has been continued by his descendents. Today, the Castle remains the Armstrong family home.

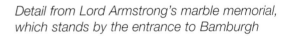

Detail from Lord Armstrong's marble memorial, which stands by the entrance to Bamburgh

Recent History

During the Second World War, Bamburgh Castle briefly saw military service once again as an Area Military Headquarters. In more recent times, the shooting has been of a more peaceable nature, the beauty and majesty of its setting having appealed to numerous film-makers. Bamburgh's 'credits' include:

Ivanhoe (1952)
El Cid (1961)
Becket (1964)
The Devils (1970)
Mary, Queen of Scots (1971)
Macbeth (1972)
The Tempest (1980)
Elizabeth (1998)

Although throughout the 19th and 20th centuries a certain amount of archaeological exploration was conducted on this most important site, it became clear that this must be planned and co-ordinated if the maximum benefit was to be realised. Accordingly, in 1996, the Bamburgh Research Project was set up to investigate the archaeology and history of the Bamburgh area, research which is ongoing.

*Bamburgh Castle by
TM Richardson Jnr. hangs
in the Crewe Museum Room*

A Tour of the Castle

Because of the number of exhibits, the notes which follow can only represent a broad overview of the various rooms. Individual items are, however, clearly labelled with, in many cases, extended explanation of their significance.

This large wooden model of the Castle built
by Mr Andrew Smith shows the end results
of Lord Armstrongs restorations

The Crewe Museum Room

The variety of the contents of this room reflects the diversity of the castle's history. This room was the medieval castle's kitchen, and the medieval masonry survives to roof height in some places. The three large fireplaces are original, as are the numerous arched doorways, which originally led to other rooms and towers of the castle. Restored by Dr John Sharp in the 18th century, this room was the main school-room of the charity school established by Lord Crewe's trustees and referred to in the History section of this book. Reminders of this are Dr Sharp's sedan chair and the impeccably neat exercise books. A large iron meat dish and ladle was probably used not only to feed the pupils but also in the Trust's infirmary.

The 7th century 'Bamburgh Beast' can be viewed through a magnifying lens. This beautiful and valuable artefact reminds us of the days when Bamburgh was the palace of the kings of Northumbria. It has been adopted as the castle's motif.

Dating from the Forsters' ownership of the castle are a dress believed to have been made for Dorothy Forster and a copy of part of the Forster family tree. The castle was purchased from the Crewe trustees in 1894 by the 1st Lord Armstrong. Exhibited paintings by the Northumbrian artist T M Richardson of Newcastle (1784-1848) and George Sykes (1863-1904) show the castle as it was prior to this time. On the far wall, a photograph taken during Lord Armstrong's restoration shows the extent of the works. Other exhibits include an oak table made from the foundations of Hadrian's bridge over the Tyne (circa AD 120) and a Minton dinner service showing the 19th century Keep. The armour is from central Asia and was presented to Lord Armstrong by Prince Boritoff, the Russian ambassador.

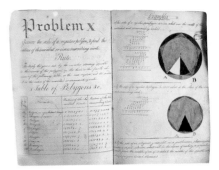

After the death of Lord Crewe in 1722 a trust was formed to help the local community. This exercise book comes from the school that was founded in the castle for the local poor children

The dress is believed to have been made for Dorothy Forster

A Minton dinner service showing the 19th century Keep

25

First Small Room

This room, together with the Second Small Room, also formed part of Dr Sharp's renovation programme. It contains a collection of largely 17th century furniture and an attractive long-case clock of 1780 by the Newcastle maker, William Fenton. Ceramics include a number of Sunderland lustre jugs and a dinner service bearing the Armstrong family crest. There are also items of glassware, silver and jewellery and an impressive pewter trencher and jug.

Of particular interest are Charles Ferguson's architectural drawings for Lord Armstrong's restoration work.

Paintings include works by English artist Peter de Wint (1784-1849) and Pietro Annigoni (1910-1988), perhaps the 20th century's most famous portrait painter.

The Second Small Room

Furnished in Napoleonic style, this room serves as a reminder that at the beginning of the 19th century the castle was prepared for possible French invasion. The prints and looking glasses are 18th century Venetian. On display are examples of 19th century Derby and continental porcelain.

The Crewe Entrance Hall

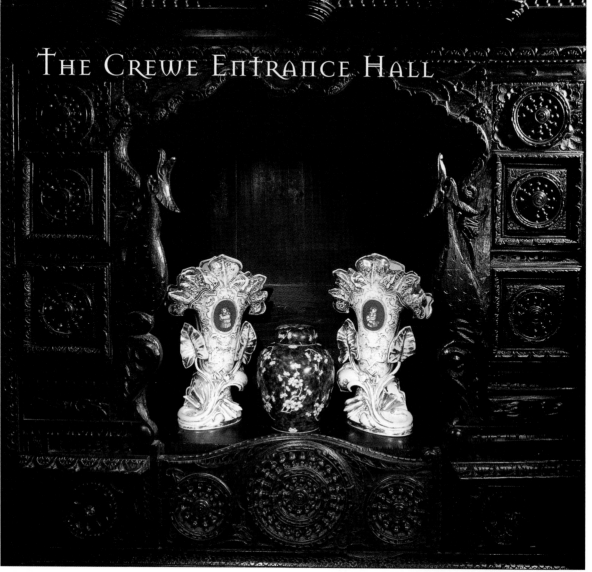

This room was restored at the end of the 19th century by Lord Armstrong and together with the previous two rooms forms the ground floor of the Crewe lodgings. The upper floors now contain two rented apartments.

Items of interest include a set of coastguard rules dated 1771. Since being granted a royal charter in 1514, Trinity House has had responsibility for the safe navigation of British coastal waters.

The Farne lighthouse of Longstone (made famous by Bamburgh's Grace Darling) was not erected until 1826 but this document shows that fifty years earlier, Dr Sharp and the Crewe trustees were taking a keen interest in the safety of local shipping. Further illustrations depict the condition of the castle prior to restoration and another architect's drawing dated 1895 shows the proposals for this submitted to Lord Armstrong. The coats of arms of Lord Crewe and Dr Sharp hang on the wall.

Lord Armstrong by a local artist

*The Farne Islands seen from the Castle,
in an unusually tranquil mood*

'An ACCOUNT of the SIGNALS made Use of at BAMBROUGH CASTLE *in the County of* Northumberland *in case Ships or Vessels are perceived in Distress, and of the charitable Institutions established there for their Assistance and Relief, now published by the Direction of the Trustees of* Nathanael *late* Lord Crewe, *with the Approbation of the Master, Pilots, and Seamen of the Trinity-house, in* Newcastle upon Tyne.'

From the set of coastguard rules dated 1771, which hang in the Entrance Hall. These rules were published some 50 years before the Farne lighthouse was built.

A plan from the Entrance Hall, showing the arrangement of chains around the Bamburgh coast. These chains, which hang in the ground floor of the keep, were used to help ships stricken on the rocks and beaches

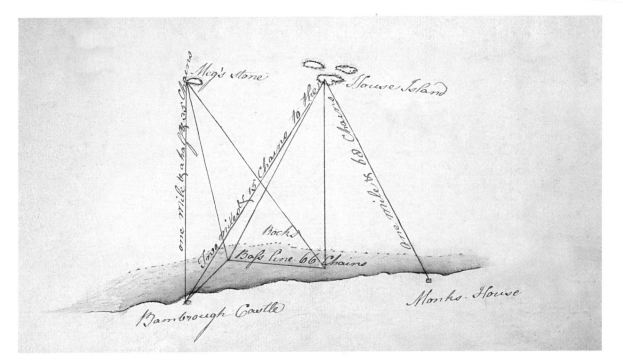

THE KING'S HALL

Entry to the King's Hall is through a medieval arch, one of three adjacent ones under the minstrels' gallery. With the exception of these, the Hall is a tribute to the skill of Victorian craftsmanship being almost entirely the product of Lord Armstrong's work at the close of the 19th century, although following the outline plan of the medieval hall. The magnificent 'false hammer-beam' roof was carved from teak over a period of years by Thomas Worsnop of Rothbury, Northumberland. The panelling is also of teak with decorative panels of pollard oak.

Much of the armour displayed in this room was loaned to the castle by the Armouries of HM The Tower of London in 1976. The remainder is from the castle's own collection, expertly restored in recent years by Mr David Oliver of Thropton in Northumberland.

A collection of fine portraits includes the 1st Lord Armstrong, Dr John Sharp, William IV, George V of Hanover and Charles II as a boy. All are clearly identified and attributed. A view of Cilgerran Castle in Wales by JMW Turner hangs next to the bay window which affords uninterrupted views of Lindisfarne and the Farne Islands.

Mounting the three steps, we enter the Cross Hall.

THE CROSS HALL

Above the Tudor-style fireplace is a copy of The Card Players by Theodor Rombouts (1597-1637), the original of which hangs in the Royal Museum, Antwerp. To the right of the fireplace is a bronze by David Rawnsley of Lady Armstrong and her children. Other paintings include a picture of the Holy Family, Il Silencio, by Marcello Venusti (1515-1579) and A View of Bamburgh Castle by Thomas Miles Richardson painted in 1845.

THE CROSS HALL

The Porch

On entering the porch we are immediately aware of the elaborately vaulted stone ceiling. The representation of knotted rope and wooden planks is believed to have been inspired by a similar design in Christ Church, Oxford. There are portraits of Lord Nathaniel Crewe, Bishop of Durham and his wife, Dorothy Forster, who was co-heir with her nephew Thomas to the Bamburgh and Blanchland estates which they inherited in 1701. There is also a portrait of her niece, sister to Thomas and also called Dorothy, famous for her rescue of her brother from Newgate Gaol. The seat covering of the Queen Anne chair was worked by Mrs Maude Forster-Gregory, a life-long resident of the castle.This porch, together with the Faire Chamber and passageway, were reconstructed by Lord Armstrong.

En-route from the Porch to the Faire Chamber is this characterful stairwell

The Faire Chamber

The windows overlooking Bamburgh village with the Cheviot Hills in the distance give this room a light and airy atmosphere enhanced by the Louis XV and XVI style chairs. There is also a sofa and set of chairs bearing the crest of the Spanish Duke of Ossuna.

This room is particularly notable for its exhibition of ceramics including examples of 18th and early 19th century decorative china, a collection of 18th century souvenir patch boxes and an exquisite Dresden dessert service. The picture of the Three Graces, painted on china, is by the Hungarian Johannes Quast.

To the left of the fireplace hangs a country scene painted by Jan Brueghel the younger (1601-1678). The portrait of Lady Derwentwater, is in the style of Sir Godfrey Kneller. At her insistence, her husband, the 3rd Earl of Derwentwater and a relative of the Forsters, joined General Tom Forster in the 1715 Jacobite uprising. He, like Tom, was captured but was not so lucky: instead of escaping, he was beheaded for treason on 24th February, 1716. It is said that her ghost can still be seen staring out of the upper windows of their home, Dilston Castle, awaiting his return.

The Passageway

On the wall hangs a French tapestry from Aubusson and in the window recess, a portrait of General Tom Forster whose rescue by his sister Dorothy has already been mentioned.

Of special interest is the door curtain made from their uniforms by Russian prisoners of the Crimean War in recognition of their humane treatment at the hands of their captors.

The Armoury

We are now on the first floor of the oldest surviving part of the castle, the Keep built in mid 12th century. The Keep was the first area to be made habitable again by Dr Sharp in the early 18th century when he created a small apartment for the use of visiting trustees. The entry into the keep has been cut through the medieval wall in the modern era. As originally built the room functioned as a chapel, but today is the Armoury. The first thing you see on entering is the suit of armour known as the Nuremberg Suit, made in Germany in the late 16th century. Around the walls, the pikes, halberds and muskets dating from the beginning of the 19th century were issued to local militia in expectation of a Napoleonic invasion.

Other items on display represent the history of projectile weapons, from a composite bow of circa 1450 through a Flemish target crossbow (circa 1650 and complete with tensioning apparatus) to firearms including a German 17th century wheellock and early matchlocks.

Lady Armstrong by Pietro Annigoni

The 4th Lord Armstrong by Judi Kent Pyrah

The Court Room

This was one of the principal rooms of the keep, probably a stateroom with an adjacent chamber. The original windows would have been much smaller than those of the present room and would have allowed the smoke from an open fire, in the centre of the room, to escape as well as allowing light in.

Nowadays it serves as a portrait gallery of the Forster, Crewe, Sharp and Armstrong families, pride of place being given to the 1972 Annigoni portrait of Maria-Teresa, 4th Lady Armstrong, as well as being home to a Sevres gold painted dinner service.

Ground Floor of the Keep

This is the very heart of the medieval fortress. The scale of the fortifications can be appreciated by the thickness of the walls, between 3 and 4 metres (see picture top right). The room, probably the guardroom, represents half of the ground floor, being separated by a strong cross-wall so that if half of the Keep were taken, defence could be maintained from the other half. The well, dating from Anglo-Saxon times and incorporated into the Keep, emphasises the importance through the ages of a reliable source of clean water to a

defensive position. Perhaps only one of several it is a remarkable feat of early engineering, being sunk through the volcanic dolerite on which the castle stands to a depth of 45 metres.

The huge chains suspended from the wall were used by Dr Sharp for the rescue and salvage of ships wrecked on the coast.

A dated signature on the wall records the visit of Queen Mary on August 20th, 1924.

Passing down a stair and corridor we come to the domestic rooms of the castle.

BAKEHOUSE

SCVLLERY

These two rooms have been restored to their early 20th century condition by castle staff and contain contemporary utensils and appliances, many of which are on loan from the Beamish Museum in County Durham. The Daisy Patent Vacuum Cleaner of 1908 provides a reminder that even castles need to be cleaned!

The arm of a stone chair, thought to be part of the throne of the Northumberland Kings

The childrens activity area in the museum

THE ARCHAEOLOGY MUSEUM

This records the work of Dr Brian-Hope Taylor in the mid 20th century and subsequent excavations by the Bamburgh Research Project. There are informative panels on Anglo-Saxon and medieval life including several illustrations prepared by the BBC's 'Meet the Ancestors' programme filmed at Bamburgh.

The display case nearest the entrance contains items that accompanied individuals buried in the Bowl Hole cemetery, located to the south of the castle. The central display case contains artefacts that illustrate the everyday life of the medieval castle. The final case contains early finds from a time when Bamburgh was the citadel of the Northumbrian kings. This includes a small gold plaque and, most fascinating of all, the arm of a stone chair, perhaps part of the throne of the Northumbrian kings.

This iron blade is all that is left of a dagger or knife which was made over 1300 years ago

The Castle Grounds

✝ THE CHAPEL

All that remains of the 12th century chapel are its foundations and the ruins of the apse at the east end. The majority of the upstanding walls represent a 19th century folly, but they give a clear indication of the extent and size of the building.

A stroll through the castle grounds reveals much of its history. The views of Lindisfarne and the Farne islands on the seaward side provide reminders of the castle's links with the early Celtic Church in Northumbria. To the landward, the strategic defensive position is revealed.

*Bamburgh Castle is one of the
few land sites where the fulmar
petrel nests*

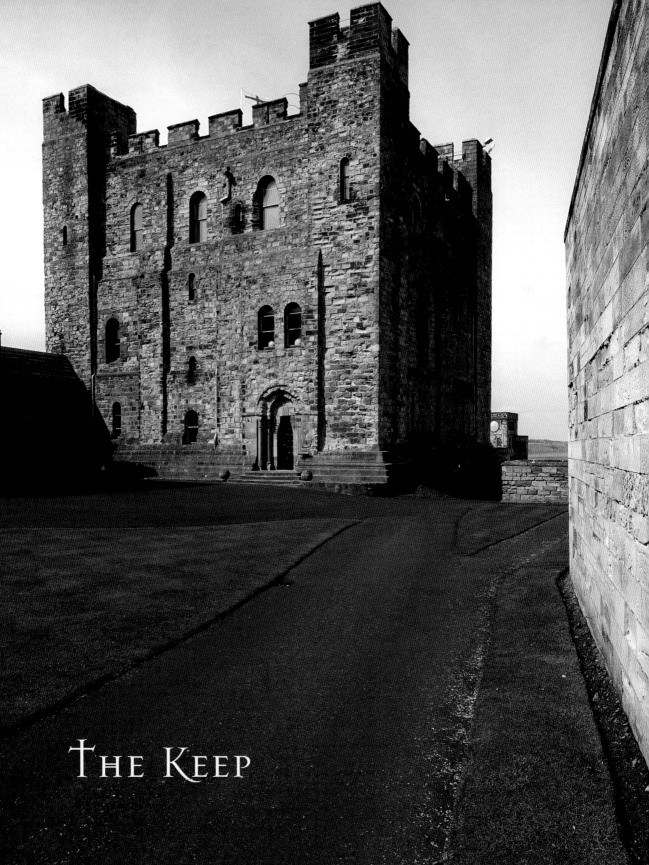

THE KEEP

The layout of the medieval castle is clear. The Keep, or donjon, stands at the junction of the Inner and East Wards. A cross wall separates the East and West Wards. The different periods of reconstruction over the last thousand years can clearly be seen in the stones of the surrounding, or curtain, wall.

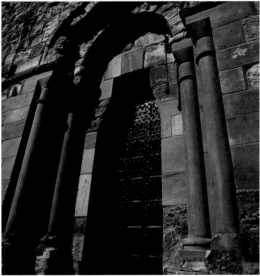

The entrance door to the Keep. Its unusual bottle-shape was so that if the outerwall was breached, retreating knights on horseback could reach the safety of the keep without dismounting

THE STABLES

Part of the stable block still gives some idea of the 19th century grandeur.
Of interest is a Victorian paupers' hearse, a further reminder of the castle's charitable connections through the Lord Crewe trustees.

The West Ward

Standing at the crosswall between the East and West Wards, we look over the site of the excavations of Dr Hope-Taylor and the Bamburgh Research Project. It was in this area that the Bamburgh Beast was discovered. The tower is the remains of the windmill constructed by Dr Sharp to grind corn for his programme of poor relief. Beyond is the narrow defile leading to St Oswald's Gate, the original, and for many hundreds of years potentially the only, entrance to the castle plateau.

Lord Armstrong
1810 - 1900

Inventor, Industrialist, Benefactor whose genius brought much employment to the North East. Enjoyment to the subsequent generations through his restoration of Bamburgh Castle and his creation of the Cragside Estate, whose house first to be lit by electricity in the world pioneered technology that emancipated so much of the world from household drudgery, and today we take for granted.

...is interred at Rothbury.

The Armstrong Museum

and the Bamburgh Castle Aviation Artefacts Museum

These are housed in the former Laundry building which preserves some original features.

The Armstrong Museum celebrates the life and work of the 1st Lord Armstrong and contains examples of the products of the various Armstrong enterprises which funded the restoration of the castle to its present form. Shipbuilding, armaments manufacture and heavy engineering are represented, together with a section on hydro-electric power for which his home, Cragside, is famous. Exhibits are clearly identified and explained.

The Armstrong Accumulator

The Aviation Artefacts Museum was put together by Mr Derek Walton of Seahouses. All the exhibits have either an Armstrong or Northumbrian connection and range from components salvaged from wrecked aircraft of the two World Wars to more modern jet engines. A separate brochure is available for this part of the museum.

A 5" Naval Gun

Bamburgh Castle

Northumberland

Home of the Armstrong Family

"The Finest Castle in England"

BAMBURGH IN HISTORY

Contents

Bamburgh in History – A Brief Overview

A Tour of the Castle

The Castle Grounds

BAMBURGH CASTLE

"THE FINEST CASTLE IN ENGLAND"

Designed and Photographed by Nick McCann

Written by Bryan Cleary

Technical Supervision - Matthew Limbert

Watercolour of Bamburgh Castle from the South

Published by Heritage House Group Ltd.
Heritage House Lodge Lane Derby DE1 3HE
Tel: 01332 347087 Fax: 01332 290688
email: publications@hhgroup.co.uk